MINNESOTA
VIKINGS

by Marty Gitlin

Published by ABDO Publishing Company, 8000 West 78th Street, Edina, Minnesota 55439. Copyright © 2011 by Abdo Consulting Group, Inc. International copyrights reserved in all countries. No part of this book may be reproduced in any form without written permission from the publisher. SportsZone™ is a trademark and logo of ABDO Publishing Company.

Printed in the United States of America,
North Mankato, Minnesota
062010
092010

Editor: Matt Tustison
Copy Editor: Nicholas Cafarelli
Interior Design and Production: Craig Hinton
Cover Design: Becky Daum

Photo Credits: Andy King/AP Images, cover; NFL Photos/AP Images, title page, 4, 7, 9, 10, 12, 20, 27, 33, 42 (middle), 42 (bottom), 43 (top); AP Images, 16, 19, 23, 24, 42 (top); Gene Herrick/AP Images, 15; Jim Mone/AP Images, 28, 43 (middle); Larry Salzman/AP Images, 31; Tom Olmscheid/AP Images, 34, 44; Tim Sharp/AP Images, 37; Morry Gash/AP Images, 38, 43 (bottom); David Stluka/AP Images, 40; Hannah Foslien/AP Images, 47

Library of Congress Cataloging-in-Publication Data
Gitlin, Marty.
  Minnesota Vikings / Marty Gitlin.
    p. cm. — (Inside the NFL)
  ISBN 978-1-61714-018-1
  1. Minnesota Vikings (Football team)—History—Juvenile literature. I. Title.
  GV956.M5G58 2010
  796.332'6409776579--dc22
                      2010017021

TABLE OF CONTENTS

THE PURPLE
PEOPLE EATERS

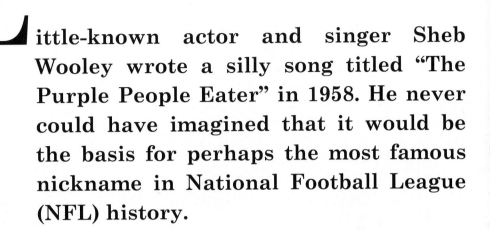

Little-known actor and singer Sheb Wooley wrote a silly song titled "The Purple People Eater" in 1958. He never could have imagined that it would be the basis for perhaps the most famous nickname in National Football League (NFL) history.

Carl Eller, Jim Marshall, Alan Page, and Gary Larsen. They were the four men on the Minnesota Vikings' defensive line in the late 1960s and early 1970s. And they were indeed known as the Purple People Eaters.

Why? Because they wore purple uniforms and they swallowed up anyone carrying a football. The Purple People Eaters were among the most dominant defensive line corps ever.

Marshall had been with the Vikings the longest. He played for the Vikings since their first season in 1961. Eller was added in 1964 and Larsen in 1965. Page came aboard in 1967.

LEFT TO RIGHT, VIKINGS DEFENSIVE LINEMEN CARL ELLER, ALAN PAGE, GARY LARSEN, AND JIM MARSHALL WERE KNOWN AS THE PURPLE PEOPLE EATERS.

FROM THE FIELD TO THE BENCH

Athletes who wonder what they will do after they retire from sports can draw inspiration from former Vikings defensive lineman Alan Page.

Page recorded 173 sacks in his career. He was selected as the NFL Most Valuable Player in 1971, a rare feat for a defensive player. But when he left the game, he did not merely look back at his achievements on the gridiron. He had already enrolled in law school at the University of Minnesota and passed his bar exam. He became so successful as a lawyer that he was elected to the Minnesota State Supreme Court in 1993. As of 2010, he was still on the court.

Page expressed his philosophy about football and its place in his life upon retirement from the sport in 1981. "It's been more than a little bit fun, more than a little bit interesting, but I guess what I'm saying is that it hasn't been all that important," he said.

Their legend began to grow toward the end of the 1960s.

When they gained experience playing together, they struck fear into running backs and quarterbacks throughout the NFL.

The Vikings' defense blossomed in 1969. The Purple People Eaters were dominant, as usual. The secondary was becoming a force, too. It featured future Hall of Fame safety Paul Krause. He had a knack for making interceptions. He had 53 of them during his 12 years with the Vikings. He finished his career with 81 interceptions, which still stands as an NFL record.

VIKINGS DEFENSIVE END JIM MARSHALL RUNS IN PURSUIT AGAINST THE LOS ANGELES RAMS IN A 1969 GAME. MARSHALL STARTED IN A THEN-RECORD 270 STRAIGHT GAMES FROM 1961 TO 1979.

During the regular season, the Vikings' defense allowed just 2,720 yards and 12 touchdowns. Opponents averaged only 9.5 points and fewer than 200 total yards per game. Minnesota surrendered 14 points or fewer in each of its final 13 regular-season games that season.

But it was not just their defense that stood out. Led by quarterback Joe Kapp, running back Dave Osborn, and wide receiver Gene Washington, Minnesota had one of the best

THE GREATEST "THIEF"

The success of Vikings safety Paul Krause was often overshadowed by that of the Purple People Eaters. Through 2009, Krause was the NFL's career leader in interceptions with 81. He wasted no time establishing himself when he led the league with 12 as a rookie with the Washington Redskins in 1964. He racked up at least five interceptions in nine of his first 12 years in the league. Krause was voted into eight Pro Bowls. He was enshrined in the Pro Football Hall of Fame in 1998.

offenses in the league, as well. The Vikings' offense compiled 4,096 yards and 39 touchdowns during the regular season. They led the NFL by scoring 379 total points. Meanwhile, the defense allowed only 133 points for the season. Needless to say, the Vikings were tough to beat.

After finishing 12–2 in the regular season, the Vikings won the Central Division and made the playoffs. They edged the visiting Los Angeles Rams 23–20 in the first round. It was the first playoff victory in team history. One week later they played host to the Cleveland Browns in the NFL Championship Game.

On January 4, 1970, with the temperature only 8 degrees, the Vikings dismantled the Browns. Kapp completed 7 of 13 passes for 169 yards and a touchdown. He rushed for another touchdown. Osborn rushed 18 times for

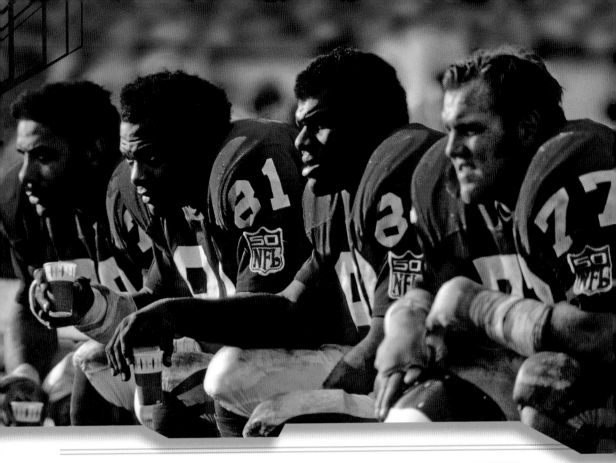

FROM *LEFT*, JIM MARSHALL, CARL ELLER, ALAN PAGE, AND GARY LARSEN—THE PURPLE PEOPLE EATERS—TAKE A BREAK.

108 yards and a touchdown, as well. Meanwhile, the Vikings' defense kept Cleveland's high-powered offense in check. The Vikings held a 27–0 lead late in the fourth quarter before Cleveland finally scored a touchdown. It was not close to enough. Minnesota won 27–7.

BAD START, BAD FINISH, GREAT MIDDLE

The 1969 Vikings experienced a rather strange regular season. They lost their first game to the New York Giants and their last game to the Atlanta Falcons. The 12 games in between? They won them all. Included was a 51–3 thrashing of the same Cleveland team they clobbered for the NFL title and a berth in the Super Bowl.

THE VIKINGS' JOE KAPP DROPS BACK TO PASS AGAINST THE CHIEFS DURING SUPER BOWL IV. KAPP THREW TWO INTERCEPTIONS IN MINNESOTA'S 23–7 LOSS.

UNORTHODOX STYLE

Vikings quarterback Joe Kapp was far from typical. He often threw off balance or on the run or even sidearm. He spent most of his career in the Canadian Football League and did not perform particularly well after joining the NFL. But he did play well in 1969. Kapp led the Vikings to 12 victories in the 13 games he played during the regular season. He threw 19 touchdown passes along the way.

Although the Vikings had won the NFL Championship Game, they were still not champions. Starting in 1966, the NFL champion began playing the American Football League (AFL) champion in the Super Bowl. To truly be champions, the Vikings needed to beat the Kansas City Chiefs in Super Bowl IV.

The Vikings were expected to dominate the game. At the time, many people considered the NFL to be superior to the AFL. However, it was the other way around in Super Bowl IV.

The Purple People Eaters were able to slow down Kansas City early on. The Chiefs did not reach the end zone for most of two quarters. But the Vikings could not stop Kansas City from scoring. Future Hall of Fame kicker Jan Stenerud made three field goals in the first half. The Chiefs finally broke through to the end zone when running back Mike Garrett added a second-quarter touchdown.

As the Chiefs' offense slowly chipped away at the Vikings, the Chiefs' defense completely shut down the Vikings' offense. Minnesota finally scored when Osborn ran five yards for a touchdown in the third quarter.

WRONG-WAY MARSHALL

Vikings defensive lineman Jim Marshall recovered an NFL-record 29 fumbles during his career. One of those fumble recoveries stands out in NFL history because of what Marshall did with the ball. In a game at San Francisco on October 25, 1964, Marshall scooped up a fumble and ran 66 yards . . . the wrong way! He reached the end zone and heaved the ball out of bounds. The result was a two-point safety for the 49ers. Marshall did make several big plays in the game, however, and the Vikings still won.

But the Chiefs had shut down the Vikings' running backs all day. The Chiefs did not let up. It did not help that Kapp threw two interceptions and the Vikings fumbled twice. The underdog Chiefs added a 46-yard touchdown pass late in the third quarter to shock the Vikings, 23–7.

The Vikings had lost their first Super Bowl. Unfortunately for the team's fans, that would soon become an all-too-familiar experience.

CHAPTER 2

GROWING INTO GREATNESS

The birth of the Vikings occurred more than a year and a half before they stepped onto the field for their first game. The NFL granted the Minneapolis-St. Paul area a franchise on January 28, 1960.

Among the first orders of business for the new team was to hire a coach. They selected recently-retired quarterback Norm Van Brocklin. Van Brocklin and general manager Bert Rose then set out to stock the squad with the best players possible.

The Vikings selected running back Tommy Mason and

FIRST THE NAME, THEN THE GAME

Minnesota general manager Bert Rose recommended that the new football team be called the Vikings. The name was soon adopted. The team was named in honor of the large number of people of Nordic descent who immigrated into that region of the country and still live there.

future Hall of Fame quarterback Fran Tarkenton in their first draft. They acquired talented

THE VIKINGS SELECTED OFFENSIVE TACKLE RON YARY FIRST OVERALL IN THE 1968 NFL/AFL DRAFT. HE WOULD PLAY 15 SEASONS FOR MINNESOTA.

QB TO COACH

The Vikings apparently believed that Norm Van Brocklin needed no seasoning to be a head coach. He ended his career as a quarterback in 1960 by leading the Philadelphia Eagles to the NFL championship and winning the Most Valuable Player (MVP) award. Nine months later, he was guiding the Vikings from the sideline.

Van Brocklin had joined the Los Angeles Rams in 1949. He led the NFL in passing yards per attempt in 1950, 1951, 1952, and 1954. He threw for a league-record 554 yards in one game in 1951. He also led the Rams to the title that year. He finished his career with 23,611 passing yards, 173 touchdown throws, and nine Pro Bowl appearances.

But he was far less successful as a coach. He finished his time with the Vikings with a 29–51–4 record. He then coached the Atlanta Falcons for seven seasons with limited success. Van Brocklin was inducted into the Pro Football Hall of Fame in 1971.

players such as offensive lineman Grady Alderman, running back Hugh McElhenny, and wide receiver Jerry Reichow from other teams. They added center Mick Tingelhoff in 1962. By 1964, all of those players had represented the Vikings in the Pro Bowl.

Despite having some talented players, the Vikings went only 3–11 in 1961. Losing records are typical for expansion teams. It often takes a few seasons for new teams to catch up to the established teams. Despite their overall record, the Vikings certainly came prepared to play in their very first game. The Chicago Bears almost always contended for an NFL title. But on this day the Vikings dominated their rivals 37–13.

Some people had thought Tarkenton was too inexperienced to play in that game.

MINNESOTA QUARTERBACK FRAN TARKENTON SCRAMBLES AGAINST THE
GREEN BAY PACKERS IN 1966.

However, he came off the bench against the Bears and threw for 250 yards and four touchdowns. He quickly took over as the starter. It was not long before Tarkenton became one of the best quarterbacks in the league.

However, it is often said that defense wins championships.

HOME SWEET HOME

The Vikings failed to win a game away from home for nearly a season and a half. They went 3–4 at home and 0–7 on the road in 1961, their first season. They then lost their first two road games in 1962 before winning in Los Angeles against the Rams, 38–14. They took the momentum and ran with it, beating the Philadelphia Eagles the next week. But they did not win another game the rest of the season.

The Vikings were going nowhere until they improved theirs.

Minnesota surrendered at least 28 points in nine of its final 13 games. They had allowed a whopping 407 for the 1961 season. The Vikings allowed nearly 30 points per game in 1962, 1963, and 1965, as well. They finally managed to put together a strong defensive season in 1964. It resulted in their first winning record at 8–5–1.

After the Vikings slid back to 7–7 in 1965 and 4–9–1 in 1966, Van Brocklin quit. He was replaced by Canadian Football League veteran coach Bud Grant.

Meanwhile, Tarkenton was traded to the New York Giants for draft picks. The picks proved very smart. They would be used to select Pro Bowl offensive linemen Ron Yary and Ed White.

As for Tarkenton? He returned to the Vikings five years later.

Grant worked wonders in Minnesota. With one game remaining in the 1968 season, the Vikings needed a win over the Philadelphia Eagles. They

BURLY BILL BROWN

Running back Bill Brown was among the most underrated players in Vikings history. The bullish 230-pounder was a consistent runner and one of the finest pass-catching backs in the NFL. He rushed for at least 600 yards in five consecutive seasons starting in 1964, when he earned the first of four trips to the Pro Bowl. He also caught more than 30 passes in four of those years. Brown's finest season by far was in 1964, when he managed career bests in rushing yards (866), catches (48), and receiving yards (703) to help the Vikings secure their first winning record.

VIKINGS RUNNING BACK BILL BROWN GIVES SON SCOTT AND DAUGHTER MICHELLE A RIDE ON HIS BACK AT HIS HOME IN 1965.

also needed Chicago to lose to Green Bay. If all that happened, they would earn their first play-off spot. The pressure became intense when the Vikings were informed that the Bears were losing.

Early in the second half, Minnesota linebacker Wally Hilgenberg forced a fumble. The Vikings recovered, and they began marching down the field.

Minnesota cashed in when quarterback Joe Kapp tossed a game-winning 30-yard touchdown pass to Gene Washington. With the Bears' loss, the Vikings were heading to the playoffs.

The Vikings traveled to Baltimore to play the Colts. The Colts had been nearly unstoppable during the regular season. They had finished 13–1. Their hot streak continued in the playoffs. Baltimore beat the Vikings 24–14.

It was a disappointing loss for the Vikings. However, during that 1968 season the Vikings had shown that they were one of the league's elite teams. There would be many more playoff celebrations—and disappointments—to come.

BUD GRANT BECAME THE VIKINGS' COACH IN 1967. THE NEXT SEASON, HE LED THE FRANCHISE TO THE PLAYOFFS FOR THE FIRST TIME.

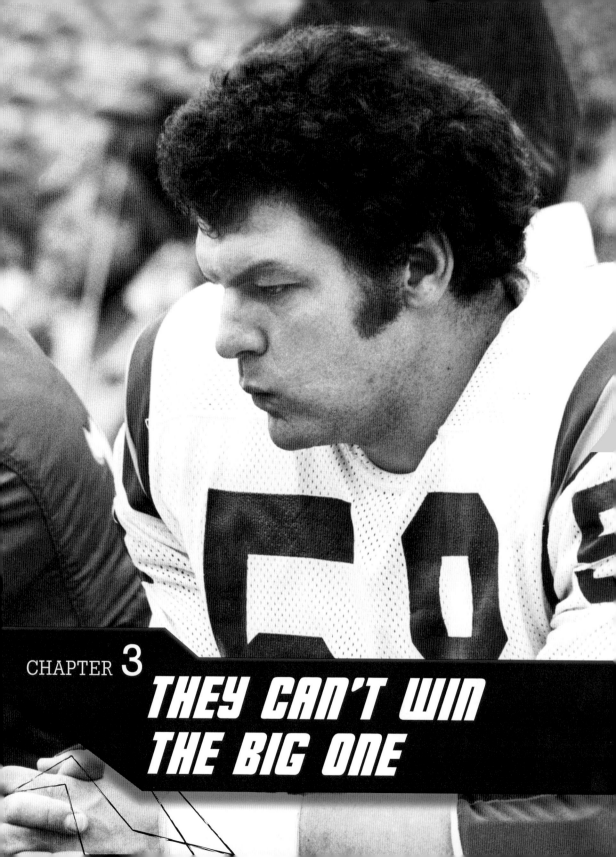

CHAPTER 3

THEY CAN'T WIN THE BIG ONE

T he Purple People Eaters peaked in the early 1970s. Fresh off the Vikings' first Super Bowl appearance, they continued to make life miserable for opposing offenses. They surrendered 20 points or fewer in every regular-season game in 1970. They did it in all but one game in 1971.

Although the defense was strong, the offense simply did not have enough talent to win playoff games against superior competition. The Vikings lost in the first round of the playoffs in both 1970 and 1971. Including the Super Bowl IV loss against Kansas City in 1969, Minnesota scored a combined 33 points in

GREAT DEAL

The Vikings traded Joe Kapp to the New England Patriots in 1970 after a contract dispute and received a first-round draft pick in 1972. That selection was used on linebacker Jeff Siemon. It was a good choice. Siemon played 11 years for the Vikings and earned spots on the Pro Bowl team in 1973, 1975, 1976, and 1977. He helped the Vikings reach two Super Bowls during his 11 years in Minnesota.

VIKING LINEBACKER WALLY HILGENBERG'S FACIAL EXPRESSION SAYS IT ALL DURING MINNESOTA'S 24–7 LOSS TO MIAMI IN SUPER BOWL VIII ON JANUARY 13, 1974.

New York Giants, Fran Tarkenton returned to Minnesota in 1972. He led the Vikings to the playoffs the next year. And this time, they began visiting the end zone more frequently.

Tarkenton threw for a combined 355 yards and three touchdowns in playoff victories over Washington and Dallas in 1973. Those thrust the Vikings back into the Super Bowl against the Miami Dolphins. Young running back Chuck Foreman also contributed greatly in those wins for Minnesota. However, the offense again sputtered with a championship on the line. The Vikings lost 24–7 to the Dolphins in Super Bowl VIII.

A nearly identical scenario frustrated the Vikings and their fans in 1974. The team waltzed

three straight playoff games from the 1969 season to 1971. All of them were losses. The Vikings boasted an impressive regular-season mark of 35–7 during those three seasons. However, they had no title to show for it.

The Vikings needed a more consistent quarterback. So they brought back an old friend. After five seasons with the

VIKINGS RUNNING BACK CHUCK FOREMAN DRAGS A BILLS DEFENDER WITH HIM ON DECEMBER 22, 1975. FOREMAN SCORED 22 TOUCHDOWNS THAT SEASON.

into the playoffs with a 10–4 record. Minnesota beat the St. Louis Cardinals and the Los Angeles Rams in the first two playoff rounds. But the offense again abandoned the Vikings in the Super Bowl. They fell 16–6 to the Pittsburgh Steelers, an emerging NFL power, in Super Bowl IX. The Vikings were held to 119 yards, including 17 rushing, against the Steelers. Tarkenton threw three interceptions in the defeat.

Minnesota continued on the same path. The Vikings won 12 of 14 regular-season games in 1975. But they fell to the underdog Dallas Cowboys 17–14 in the first round of the playoffs. Minnesota then went 11–2–1 in 1976. The Vikings performed well in that season's playoffs.

They defeated the Washington Redskins 35–20 and the Los Angeles Rams 24–13 to qualify for their fourth Super Bowl in eight seasons.

The Vikings' Super Bowl frustration, however, reached a boiling point when they lost 32–14 to the Oakland Raiders

DID DREW PUSH OFF?

One of the most controversial plays in Vikings history occurred in the NFC first-round playoff game against Dallas on December 28, 1975. The Vikings led 14–10 when Cowboys quarterback Roger Staubach fired a 50-yard "Hail Mary" touchdown pass to wide receiver Drew Pearson with 24 seconds left. Vikings fans and players have claimed that Pearson pushed Minnesota defensive back Nate Wright on the play to help secure the catch. They say Pearson should have been called for offensive pass interference. Pearson has denied that contention. Dallas won 17–14.

DREW PEARSON OUTMANEUVERS THE VIKINGS' PAUL KRAUSE (22) AND NATE WRIGHT (43) FOR A CONTROVERSIAL TOUCHDOWN CATCH IN THE COWBOYS' 17–14 VICTORY IN THE 1975 PLAYOFFS.

LITTLE EMOTION, BIG WINNER

Bud Grant stood stoically on the sidelines when he coached the Vikings. He rarely cracked a smile or spoke with emotion to the media or his players after games. He shared authority with his assistant coaches. But he knew how to win.

Though Grant's teams lost four Super Bowls, they suffered through no losing seasons from 1968 to 1978. The Vikings qualified for the playoffs in 10 of those 11 years. Quarterback Fran Tarkenton spoke glowingly about his coach, with whom he enjoyed his best seasons.

"The players and coaches all knew who was in charge," said Tarkenton, who won the NFL Most Valuable Player award in 1975. "...Bud let everyone do their job and respected them as a professional. It was an atmosphere ripe for individual and team success; everyone was motivated by his confidence in them."

in Super Bowl XI on January 9, 1977. After all, their defense had not given up that many points in a game in four seasons. The national media criticized their performance.

"The football game was essentially over [by halftime], as so many Super Bowls have been concluded prematurely by the Vikings, who somehow seem to save their worst for [Super Bowl games]," wrote Dan Jenkins of *Sports Illustrated*. "The only fascinating part was how ingeniously easy Minnesota made it for the Oakland Raiders this time."

Through the 2009 season, the Vikings had not made it back to the Super Bowl. The Vikings team that lost to Oakland in Super Bowl XI was getting old. Linebacker Wally Hilgenberg, safety Paul Krause, Tarkenton, Foreman, and all four

OAKLAND LINEMAN OTIS SISTRUNK PURSUES MINNESOTA QUARTERBACK
FRAN TARKENTON IN SUPER BOWL XI. THE VIKINGS LOST 32–14.

Purple People Eaters had left the Vikings or retired by 1979.

The Vikings lost to Dallas in the second round of the 1977 playoffs. They lost to Los Angeles in the first round in 1978. The Vikings combined for just 16 points in the two games. An era of greatness was over. The ultimate goal of winning a Super Bowl was not achieved. But more success was on the way. And so was one of the most stunning trades in NFL history.

CHAPTER 4

BAD DEAL OF THE CENTURY

By the 1980s, the Purple People Eaters were gone and the fans were blue. The defense that had terrorized opponents for more than a decade had become quite ordinary. So had the entire team.

Even the coach had changed—twice. Bud Grant retired in 1984 and was replaced by assistant Les Steckel. Grant then returned for one year in 1985 after the Vikings set team records by giving up 484 points and losing 13 games in the 1984 season.

THE GRAND UNVEILING

The Vikings played their first regular-season game at the brand-new Metrodome on September 12, 1982. They marked the occasion with a 17–10 victory over the Tampa Bay Buccaneers. Unfortunately, that season was damaged by a labor dispute between NFL players and owners that resulted in a work stoppage. Play was halted between mid-September and mid-November, shortening the season to nine games.

HERSCHEL WALKER HOLDS UP HIS NEW MINNESOTA JERSEY AFTER HE WAS ACQUIRED FROM DALLAS IN 1989. THE TRADE WAS A DISASTER FOR THE VIKINGS.

The next coach was far more successful. Jerry Burns guided the Vikings into the playoffs after the 1987 season. The Vikings won on the road over the New Orleans Saints and the San Francisco 49ers to get to the NFC Championship Game against the Washington Redskins. However, a fifth Super Bowl berth was denied when the Vikings lost to the host Redskins 17–10.

THAT'S BETTER!

Through 2009, only one Viking had earned an NFL Comeback Player of the Year award. The award is given to the established player who returns from a bad or injury-hampered year with the greatest success. That player was quarterback Tommy Kramer in 1986. Kramer was miserable in 1985, leading the league in interceptions with 26. But he bounced back to have his best season in 1986. He tossed 24 touchdown passes with just 10 interceptions. His quarterback rating, which takes into consideration many passing statistics, jumped from 67.8 in 1985 to a career-best 92.6 in 1986.

The Vikings returned to the playoffs again after the 1988 season. They advanced to the second round before falling to the powerful 49ers 34–9 in San Francisco.

The Vikings were in need of some new faces. Quarterback Wade Wilson did not produce statistics that amazed anyone. The team boasted virtually no running game. Wide receiver Anthony Carter and tight end Steve Jordan were the Vikings' only receiving threats. Led by defensive end Chris Doleman, linebacker Scott Studwell, safety Joey Browner, and cornerback Carl Lee, the defense was strong. But it did not play at a Purple People Eaters-like level.

Five games into the 1989 season, Vikings general manager Mike Lynn decided that one great running back was all that

COACH LES STECKEL, *RIGHT*, AND QUARTERBACK TOMMY KRAMER REACT DURING MINNESOTA'S 42–13 LOSS TO SAN DIEGO IN THE 1984 OPENER.

stood between his team and a Super Bowl championship. So he made one of the most significant and controversial trades in NFL history.

The Vikings acquired running back Herschel Walker from Dallas for five players—among them standout linebacker Jesse Solomon—and several

THE SACK MAN

Chris Doleman was a fixture at defensive end for the Vikings from 1985 to 1993. He also played for the team in 1999, his final NFL season. He was among the top tacklers in the league. He recorded more than 100 tackles in 1985 and 1991. But his finest attribute was as a pass rusher. Doleman led the NFL in sacks with 21 in 1989. He finished his career with 150.5. Through 2009, that ranked fourth in NFL history. Doleman racked up at least 10 sacks in eight seasons in his NFL career.

THE "BLACK AND BLUE" DIVISION

From the moment they entered the NFL, the Vikings established rivalries with teams in their geographical region—the Chicago Bears, the Detroit Lions, and the Green Bay Packers. When the NFL merged with the American Football League in 1970, those four teams were placed in the Central Division of the NFC. It became known as the "Black and Blue" division for the rough style of play exhibited by all four teams, particularly when they played against each other.

The head-to-head series between those teams have been marked by aggressive defense. In recent years, however, the Packers and Vikings have become better known for their offenses. Through the 2009 season, the Vikings had winning records (including playoff games) against Detroit (65–30–2) and Chicago (52–44–2) and had played Green Bay (48–49–1) nearly even.

draft picks. This included three picks in the first round and three in the second round. The football world was stunned.

The deal would become a disaster. Walker had rushed for 1,514 yards for the Cowboys in 1988. But he played just two and a half years with the Vikings and never gained 1,000 yards in a season. Minnesota compiled a 21–23 record with Walker and then released him.

Walker ended up in Philadelphia, where he exceeded 1,000 rushing yards in his first season with the Eagles. The Cowboys, meanwhile, could not have been happier with the trade. They used the draft picks wisely to build a three-time Super Bowl champion.

"You can't blame Herschel," Carter said near the 20-year anniversary of the infamous

THE 49ERS' CHARLES HALEY (94) MOVES IN TO STOP THE VIKINGS' HERSCHEL WALKER IN SAN FRANCISCO'S 41–13 PLAYOFF WIN IN JANUARY 1990.

swap. "The ball was in Mike Lynn's hands, and it was one of the horrible trades in sports history. All the blame for that goes on one individual, and that's Mike Lynn. Sorry to say that, but it's the honest-to-God's truth."

The Vikings needed a positive change. And they got one when they hired a college coach named Dennis Green to coach the team in 1992.

CHAPTER 5

THE GREEN TEAM AND BEYOND

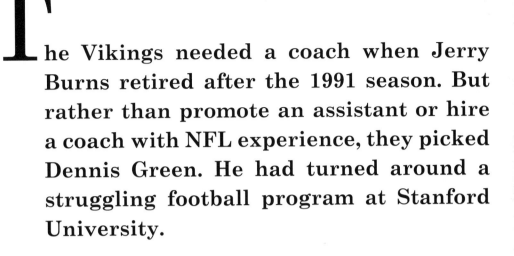

The Vikings needed a coach when Jerry Burns retired after the 1991 season. But rather than promote an assistant or hire a coach with NFL experience, they picked Dennis Green. He had turned around a struggling football program at Stanford University.

The positive effect was immediate. The Vikings won all four exhibition games in 1992 and sprinted to a 5–1 record to start the regular season. They were playing well on the field and enjoying themselves off it.

"He brought us a rebirth," defensive back Todd Scott said. "When you look at where we are,

look at Dennis Green first. He's responsible for the change."

So was a new core of players. The disastrous trade for Herschel Walker eliminated a number of draft choices. But the Vikings still managed to add talent. They signed wide receiver Cris Carter in 1990. He had been released by the Eagles.

DENNIS GREEN, SHOWN IN 1999, COACHED THE VIKINGS FROM 1992 TO 2001. THE TEAM MADE THE PLAYOFFS EIGHT TIMES IN HIS 10 SEASONS IN CHARGE.

Carter became among the best at his position throughout the 1990s.

The Vikings picked running back Terry Allen in the ninth round of the 1991 draft. He became a cornerstone of the ground game. He rushed for 1,201 yards and 13 touchdowns in 1992.

Also, Randall McDaniel and Gary Zimmerman proved to be two of the best offensive linemen in the NFL for more than a decade. And a defensive line led by Chris Doleman, Henry Thomas, and emerging star John Randle was racking up sacks.

Green guided the Vikings into the playoffs in eight of his first nine seasons. However, it seemed nothing had changed. Minnesota still played poorly in the postseason. The team was eliminated in the first round after the 1992, 1993, 1994, and 1996 seasons. The Vikings made it to the second round after the 1997 season before falling.

In 1998, however, the Vikings appeared ready to take a trip to their fifth Super Bowl. An offense led by quarterback Randall Cunningham, running back Robert Smith, receivers Carter and a rookie named Randy Moss rolled over almost every defense it faced. The Vikings scored 556 points that season, an average of 34.8 per game. It remained the most points scored in a season

GREAT GUARD

The Vikings have been fortunate to have some of the finest offensive linemen in NFL history, including Ron Yary, Gary Zimmerman, and Mick Tingelhoff. But none performed better for a longer period than Randall McDaniel. McDaniel started 15 of 16 games as a rookie in 1988. He then embarked on a run of 12 consecutive Pro Bowl seasons. During that time, he was named to nine All-Pro teams. He was enshrined in the Pro Football Hall of Fame in 2009.

ROOKIE WIDE RECEIVER RANDY MOSS HELPED THE 1998 VIKINGS SET AN NFL SINGLE-SEASON RECORD WITH 556 POINTS.

by one team in NFL history until New England surpassed it in 2007. The Vikings finished the regular season 15–1.

The Vikings continued to dominate with a 41–21 win over the Arizona Cardinals in the first round of the playoffs. But in the NFC Championship Game, the defense let them down. Cunningham played well. But Minnesota allowed Atlanta Falcons quarterback Chris Chandler to throw for 340 yards and three touchdowns. And when Falcons place-kicker Morten Andersen booted a 38-yard field goal in overtime, the Vikings experienced a crushing defeat, 30–27.

"We had such tremendous expectations," Minnesota kicker Gary Anderson said. "That makes it 10 times more disappointing."

GARY ANDERSON REACTS AFTER HE MISSED A 38-YARD FIELD-GOAL TRY LATE IN THE 1998 NFC CHAMPIONSHIP GAME AGAINST ATLANTA.

Anderson had made all 35 field goals he had attempted during the regular season. But with a little less than three minutes left and the Vikings up by seven, Anderson missed a field goal that likely would have sealed the win. The 38-yard attempt sailed wide by about a foot. Because of the miss, Atlanta was able to drive down the field and score the touchdown that forced overtime.

More heartache soon followed. Things were shaping up nicely two seasons later for the Vikings. They went 11–5 to win the NFC Central. Led by second-year quarterback Daunte Culpepper, they easily beat the New Orleans Saints 34–16 in the divisional round of the playoffs.

Then came the NFC Championship Game against the New York Giants. The Giants crushed the visiting Vikings 41–0. It was a loss that perhaps equaled the Super Bowl defeats in terms of humiliation.

The Vikings reached the playoffs after the 2004 and 2008 seasons but were eliminated by the Philadelphia Eagles both times. The team had hired coach Brad Childress in 2006 to turn things around. By 2009, they were almost there.

The Vikings were in need of a boost before the 2009 season. The team had acquired many talented players who had guided the team to the 2008 playoffs. But many fans believed the team needed a star quarterback to get them over the hump. The team got that quarterback. It was one few Vikings fans ever could have imagined to see in purple.

TRAGEDY

The Vikings received a horrible emotional blow during training camp in 2001 when Pro Bowl offensive tackle Korey Stringer collapsed and died during a workout. Sweltering temperatures on that August day in Mankato, Minnesota, played a role in his death. Doctors said he died because of heat stroke. The heat index—a combination of temperature and humidity—had reached 110 degrees that morning.

Brett Favre had played for the rival Green Bay Packers for 16 seasons before joining the New York Jets in 2008. Favre was a constant thorn in the Vikings' side while with the Packers. But Vikings fans gladly welcomed the legendary quarterback in 2009. After the 2009 season, he was the league's all-time leader in touchdown passes (497) and passing yards (69,329).

The Vikings rolled into the playoffs in 2009 behind Favre, running back Adrian Peterson, and defensive end Jared Allen.

QUARTERBACK BRETT FAVRE AND RUNNING BACK ADRIAN PETERSON
PROVIDED THE VIKINGS WITH A POWERFUL ONE-TWO PUNCH IN 2009.

END OF AN ERA

Fans and the Vikings' management grew impatient with the inability of Dennis Green to coach the team to a Super Bowl. When Minnesota showed signs of faltering in 2001, he was fired. Green had not coached the Vikings to a losing season until that year. But with the team in the process of going 5–11, he was replaced before the last game by assistant Mike Tice. The Vikings went 6–10 in Tice's first full season.

A fifth Super Bowl appearance again looked possible after a 34–3 drubbing of the Dallas Cowboys in the divisional round.

The Vikings and the New Orleans Saints had been the top teams in the NFC all season. They met in the NFC Championship Game in New Orleans.

Minnesota played well all game but was plagued by turnovers. The Vikings lost three fumbles and Favre threw two interceptions. Still, the game was tied 28–28 late in the fourth quarter. As time ran down, Favre drove the Vikings into field-goal range. However, a costly penalty pushed them back. Then New Orleans' Tracy Porter intercepted a Favre pass to end the threat. The Saints won 31–28 in overtime and then won the Super Bowl two weeks later.

"We really gave those guys the game," Peterson said. "Too many turnovers. It's eating me up inside."

Like so many times before, the Vikings fell just short. But with a strong core of players, the Vikings are hoping that next time they can make it all the way to the Super Bowl—and finally come home victorious.

THE BEST BACK IN FOOTBALL?

Many NFL experts believed Adrian Peterson would be a special player when the Vikings selected the former University of Oklahoma standout with the seventh overall pick in the 2007 NFL Draft. But he has even exceeded expectations.

Peterson immediately established himself as one of the best running backs in the league. He earned a Pro Bowl spot as a rookie by rushing for 1,341 yards. He then led the NFL with 1,760 rushing yards in 2008 and in touchdowns with 18 in 2009.

After shredding Cleveland in the 2009 opener with Browns legendary running back Jim Brown in attendance, Peterson was asked whether he was the NFL's best current back. He took it a step further.

"I want people to remember me as the best player to ever play the game," he said. "When you think about football, I want my name to pop up in your head."

TIMELINE

1960 — The NFL grants the Minneapolis-St. Paul area a franchise on January 28. Bert Rose is later named general manager and Norm Van Brocklin the first coach of the new Minnesota Vikings.

1961 — The Vikings stun the Chicago Bears 37–13 on September 17 in their first regular-season game but win just two more games the rest of the season.

1964 — The Vikings win their final three games to earn their first winning season.

1967 — Van Brocklin resigns as coach in February after a 4–9–1 season in 1966. Bud Grant takes the reins. The Purple People Eaters defense of Carl Eller, Jim Marshall, Gary Larsen, and Alan Page is in place.

1968 — The Vikings earn their first division title and playoff spot with a 24–17 defeat of Philadelphia and a loss by Chicago to Green Bay on December 15.

1970 — With their first two playoff game victories, the Vikings earn a Super Bowl berth. However, they are upset by Kansas City 23–7 on January 11.

1974 — The Vikings fall in their second Super Bowl, 24–7 to Miami on January 13.

1975 — For the second consecutive year, the Vikings lose in a Super Bowl. They fall 16–6 to Pittsburgh on January 12.

1977	The Vikings lose their fourth Super Bowl game in eight years with a 32–14 defeat to Oakland on January 9.
1982	The Vikings leave Metropolitan Stadium and open the enclosed Metrodome with a 17–10 win over Tampa Bay on September 12.
1984	Bud Grant retires as coach on January 27. He is replaced by Les Steckel, who lasts one year and is replaced by Grant for one year. Jerry Burns takes over in 1986.
1988	The Vikings reach the NFC title game for the first time since 1977 but fall 17–10 to Washington on January 17.

1989	The Vikings make an ill-fated trade with Dallas for running back Herschel Walker, swapping six early draft choices in the process.
1992	Dennis Green is hired as coach on January 10, setting off an era of excellence for the Vikings.

1999	The Vikings win 15 of 16 games and set a league record by scoring 556 points during the 1998 regular season. But they lose 30–27 to Atlanta in overtime in the NFC Championship Game on January 17.
2001	Green leads the Vikings to another NFC title game. But they lose 41–0 to the New York Giants on January 14.
2010	Quarterback Brett Favre leads the Vikings back to the NFC title game. But the Vikings turn the ball over five times in a 31–28 overtime loss to New Orleans on January 24.

QUICK STATS

FRANCHISE HISTORY

1961–

SUPER BOWLS
(wins in bold)

1969 (IV), 1973 (VIII), 1974 (IX), 1976 (XI)

NFL CHAMPIONSHIP GAMES
(1961–69; wins in bold)

1969

NFC CHAMPIONSHIP GAMES
(since 1970 AFL-NFL merger)

1973, 1974, 1976, 1977, 1987, 1998, 2000, 2009

DIVISION CHAMPIONSHIPS
(since 1970 AFL-NFL merger)

1970, 1971, 1973, 1974, 1975, 1976, 1977, 1978, 1980, 1989, 1992, 1994, 1998, 2000, 2008, 2009

KEY PLAYERS
(position, seasons with team)

Cris Carter (WR, 1990–2001)
Chris Doleman (DE; 1985–93, 1999)
Carl Eller (DE, 1964–78)
Chuck Foreman (RB, 1973–79)
Paul Krause (S, 1968–79)
Jim Marshall (DE, 1961–79)
Randall McDaniel (G, 1988–99)
Randy Moss (WR, 1998–2004)
Alan Page (DT, 1967–78)
Adrian Peterson (RB, 2007–)
John Randle (DT, 1990–2000)
Robert Smith (RB, 1993–2000)
Fran Tarkenton (QB; 1961–66, 1972–78)
Mick Tingelhoff (C, 1962–78)
Ron Yary (OT, 1968–81)
Gary Zimmerman (OT, 1986–92)

KEY COACHES

Bud Grant (1967–83, 1985): 158–96–5; 10–12 (playoffs)
Dennis Green (1992–2001): 97–62–0; 4–8 (playoffs)

HOME FIELDS

Hubert H. Humphrey Metrodome (1982–)
Metropolitan Stadium (1961–81)

* All statistics through 2009 season

QUOTES AND ANECDOTES

In the 1970s, the Vikings twice threatened to become the second team in NFL history to complete a regular season unbeaten. They fell short both times. Miami achieved that rare feat in 1972, and then finished the job by becoming the only team to ever remain undefeated through the playoffs and the Super Bowl. The Vikings won their first nine games in 1973 before they fell to Atlanta. They sprinted out to a 10–0 record in 1975 before they lost to Washington. They did win all their home games in both those seasons, however. In 1998, the Vikings finished with a franchise-best 15–1 record. Their one loss that regular season came in their eighth game, 27–24 to Tampa Bay.

NFL punters and place-kickers of the late 1970s and early 1980s had to be a bit nervous when they saw Vikings linebacker Matt Blair across the field waiting for the ball to be snapped. Blair was a standout player. Through 2009, he ranked second in franchise history with 1,452 tackles. He earned six trips to the Pro Bowl. But his specialty was blocking kicks. He recorded a franchise-record 20.5 blocks during his career.

Pro Football Hall of Fame quarterback Warren Moon played three seasons with the Vikings after a standout tenure with the Houston Oilers. He threw for 8,492 yards and 51 touchdowns in his first two years with Minnesota and earned trips to the Pro Bowl in 1994 and 1995.

When opposing quarterbacks line up under center, they know that it is quite likely they will either be harassed or sacked by defensive end Jared Allen. The Vikings obtained him in a trade with Kansas City before the 2008 season after he led the league with 15.5 sacks. He added 14.5 sacks in each of his first two years with Minnesota. He earned All-Pro status in 2007, 2008, and 2009.

GLOSSARY

berth

A place, spot, or position, such as in the NFL playoffs.

blossom

To quickly or gradually become a much better player.

contract

A binding agreement about, for example, years of commitment by a football player in exchange for a given salary.

draft

A system used by professional sports leagues to select new players in order to spread incoming talent among all teams.

enshrine

To be placed into, such as the Pro Football Hall of Fame.

expansion

In sports, to add a franchise or franchises to a league.

franchise

An entire sports organization, including the coaches, players, and staff.

momentum

A continued strong performance based on recent success.

rookie

A first-year professional athlete.

secondary

The defensive players who line up behind the linebackers to defend the pass and assist with run coverage.

sidearm

The release of a ball from the side of the body.

FOR MORE INFORMATION

Further Reading

Bruton, James. *A Tradition of Purple: An Inside Look at the Minnesota Vikings.* St. Louis Park, MN: Sports Publishing, 2007.

Klobuchar, Jim. *Purple Hearts and Golden Memories: 35 Years With the Minnesota Vikings.* Coal Valley, IL: Quality Sports Publications, 1995.

Reusse, Patrick. *Minnesota Vikings: The Complete Illustrated History.* Osceola, WI: MVP Books, 2010.

Web Links

To learn more about the Minnesota Vikings, visit ABDO Publishing Company online at **www.abdopublishing.com**. Web sites about the Vikings are featured on our Book Links page. These links are routinely monitored and updated to provide the most current information available.

Places to Visit

Mall of America Field at the Hubert H. Humphrey Metrodome
900 South 5th Street
Minneapolis, MN 55415
612-335-3336
www.msfc.com
The Vikings play their exhibition, regular-season, and playoff games here.

Minnesota State University, Mankato
170 Stadium Road
Mankato, MN 56001
952-828-6500
www.vikings.com/schedule/training-camp/index.html
This is the site of the Vikings' annual training camp, which is located 90 minutes south of the Minneapolis-St. Paul area.

Pro Football Hall of Fame
2121 George Halas Dr., NW
Canton, OH 44708
330-456-8207
www.profootballhof.com
This hall of fame and museum highlights the greatest players and moments in the history of the National Football League. Fifteen people affiliated with the Vikings are enshrined, including Bud Grant, Randall McDaniel, and Fran Tarkenton.

INDEX

About the Author

Marty Gitlin is a freelance writer based in Cleveland, Ohio. He has written more than 25 educational books, including many sports titles. Gitlin has won more than 45 awards during his 25 years as a writer, including first place for general excellence from the Associated Press. He lives with his wife and three children.